Confucius
Chinese Philosopher

Wendy Conklin, M.A.
and Gisela Lee, M.A.

Publishing Credits

Associate Editor
Christina Hill, M.A.

Assistant Editor
Torrey Maloof

Editorial Assistants
Kathryn R. Kiley
Judy Tan

Editorial Director
Emily R. Smith, M.A.Ed.

Editor-in-Chief
Sharon Coan, M.S.Ed.

Creative Director
Lee Aucoin

Cover Designer
Lesley Palmer

Designers
Deb Brown
Zac Calbert
Amy Couch
Robin Erickson
Neri Garcia

Publisher
Rachelle Cracchiolo, M.S.Ed.

Teacher Created Materials
5301 Oceanus Drive
Huntington Beach, CA 92649-1030
http://www.tcmpub.com
ISBN 978-0-7439-0437-7

Printed in China 51497

Table of Contents

Confucius in Confusing Times

Confucius (kuhn-FYOO-shuhs) was a man who lived long ago in China. He grew up during a time of war and **chaos** (KAY-aws). In spite of this, the Chinese made great advances during that time.

Great thinkers called philosophers (fuh-LAWS-uh-fuhrz) wondered about their laws. They questioned, "Is this really right?" They made others question, too. Because of this, the Chinese gained new ideas about how to live.

▼ Followers of Confucius today

Confucius was one of these thinkers. He changed and shaped Chinese culture. His teachings have influenced (IN-floo-uhntzd) people for a long time. In fact, there are some who still follow his ideas today.

Did You Know?

Today, you can read Confucius's sayings inside fortune cookies. Fortune cookies were invented in the United States. They were first seen in the 1800s.

What Did Confucius Look Like?

Confucius was a very large man. He had a beard, large teeth that hung over his lips, and warts on his nose. Even though he was funny looking, stories tell us that he was very charming.

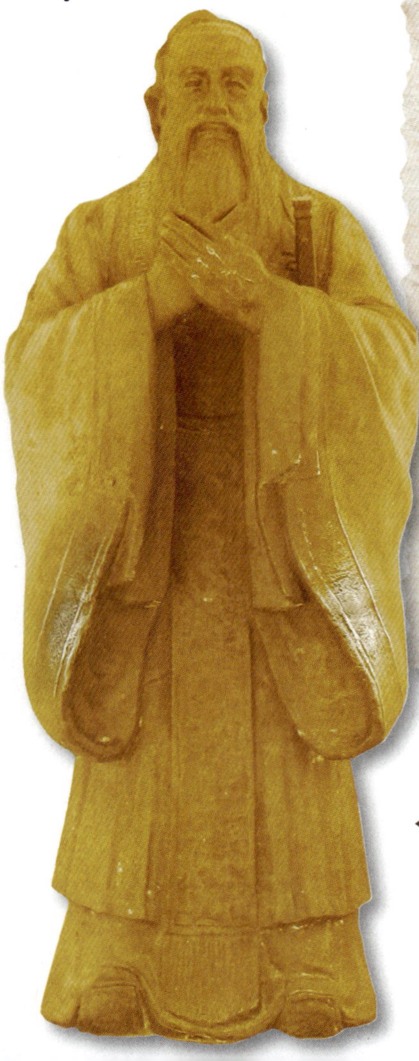

◀ Statues of Confucius are seen all over the world.

Preparing for a Downfall

King Wu
Zhou Dynasty

A long time ago, the Chinese ruled in **dynasties** (DI-nuhs-teez). This meant that all the rulers came from one family. When one person died, another was waiting to take over the job. The dynasties took on the families' names. One family could rule for hundreds of years this way. In fact, the Zhou (JO) family ruled for more than 900 years!

The Zhou-dynasty rulers were smart. They decided to unite all of China under one ruler. To make it easy to govern, they set up small **feudal** (FYOO-duhl) states. They had the workers to build good roads and canals. Everyone used the same currency. They even spoke the same language.

Most would think this would lead to a **harmonious** (hawr-MOW-nee-uhs) country. But after many years, the states started fighting. **Civil war** spread and many died. It was around this time that Confucius was born.

Ancient Chinese money

Time Line of Key Chinese Dynasties

Xia dynasty	2000–1600 B.C.
Shang dynasty	1600–1046 B.C.
Zhou dynasty	1046–221 B.C.
Western Zhou	1046–771 B.C.
Eastern Zhou	770–221 B.C.
Qin dynasty	221–206 B.C.
Han dynasty	206 B.C.–A.D. 220
Sui dynasty	A.D. 581–618
Tang dynasty	A.D. 618–907
Song dynasty	A.D. 960–1279
Yuan dynasty	A.D. 1279–1368
Ming dynasty	A.D. 1368–1644
Qing dynasty	A.D. 1644–1911

A Mandate

The first emperor of China did not like anything that challenged his rule. Any writings or books that did not agree with his ideas were destroyed. He was influenced by something called the Mandate of Heaven. He believed that if heaven was happy with him, he would rule for a long time.

A Different China Today

Since the fall of the last dynasty, China is no longer led by an emperor. Instead, a **premier** is the leader of the country today. The premier is selected by officials within the Chinese government.

◀ The Chinese premier is important in world politics.

The Young Kong

In 551 B.C., a baby was named Kong Qui (KUNG CHYOH). When this baby grew up, he was called Kung Fu-tzu (KUNG-fuh-dzu), which means Master Kong. After his death, he was known as Confucius.

Confucius was born in the feudal state of Lu. Lu was a little town in today's Shandong (SHAWN-dong) Province. Today, Lu is called Quju.

◄ Learning was important to Confucius.

▼ Shandong today

Stories say that Confucius's father was 70 years old and died when Confucius was just three. His mother, a peasant girl, was the one who raised him. In times past, his **ancestors** (AN-ses-tuhrz) had been of the noble class. But the family had lost their wealth and ended up very poor.

Early on, Confucius loved books and learning. He did not go to school. Some historians think Confucius might have had a tutor at one point. But, most everything he knew, he learned on his own.

A Job for a Teenager

Confucius worked to help support his family. He managed a **granary** for a while. He also took care of animals on grazing lands. At some point, he married and had a son and daughter.

What's in a Name?

It was not until 2000 years after his birth that Kong Qui was called Confucius. Missionaries who had traveled to the region gave him that name.

Choosing the Right Path

China's history fascinated Confucius. He read all sorts of books about China. These books helped him think of ways his government could be better. The end of the Zhou dynasty caused an **upheaval** (uhp-HEEV-uhl) in China. Confucius watched it happen. He observed how the poor lived. He watched as their harvests failed. He saw the government abuse its power. Confucius wanted to help those in need. He wanted to end wars and fighting. He devoted his life to this cause.

Wanting to change things, he hoped for a job in the government. But, Confucius could not get the job he wanted. No one in the government

▲ Bamboo fans were also used to share writing.

This book shows Confucius and his followers.

would listen to him. They were not interested in **virtue** (VUHR-chew). They knew Confucius's ideas would ruin the way they lived. So, Confucius talked to those around him about his thoughts.

Books Back Then

Back when Confucius lived, books were not like they are today. Paper had not been invented yet. So, books were made from bamboo strips. Leather bound them together in an accordion.

Dangerous Thoughts

Some think that Confucius spoke out too much and that is why he could not get a job. The government did not want to hire people with very different ideas. Leaders were afraid of change. Most leaders **inherited** (in-HAIR-uht-id) their positions. They wanted to enjoy their lives and expand their power.

Bamboo is an important food for pandas.

Scholar and Teacher

Confucius decided to start a school. He invited both nobles and peasants to learn. This was unheard of back then. "Only nobles could be educated!" the people thought. But Confucius knew that schooling would make people equal. He had only one requirement for his students. They had to love learning.

He taught his students that the government should help everyone have better lives. That was the job of the government. He thought that the government should especially take care of the young and old.

▼ Confucius teaching his students

Temple of Confucius in Quju, China

Walk on Your Side of the Street!

While governing Lu, Confucius set some interesting laws. For example, he made men and women walk on different sides of the street.

Safe in the City of Lu

The people responded well to Confucius's rules. There was less crime in the city. People could leave their doors open. Businesses stopped cheating their customers.

Confucius told his students to speak out against dishonest rulers. One ruler asked Confucius how to find honest workers. Confucius said, "Be honest yourself." Because he spoke his mind, many rulers did not like him.

Finally, a prince decided Confucius could govern the feudal state of Lu. Confucius felt that his dream of saving China was coming true at last.

Today, people in China still take care of the young and old.

On the Road Again

The dream of saving China was short-lived. Three powerful families did not like Confucius. They plotted against him.

Confucius felt that the princes had no **morals** (MOWR-uhlz). This upset Confucius. At age 54, he quit his teaching job and set out to test his ideas and beliefs.

Confucius traveled all over eastern China. He hoped to find rulers who would listen to him. He did not think that they had to lose their power. He said the leaders could share the power with the people under them to run the government. These people would know the real needs of their subjects. So, everyone would have better lives.

He found some rulers who invited him into their courts. They listened to him, but they did not give him any power. They were still afraid his ideas would cost them their own power. Other rulers simply ignored him. That hurt Confucius the most.

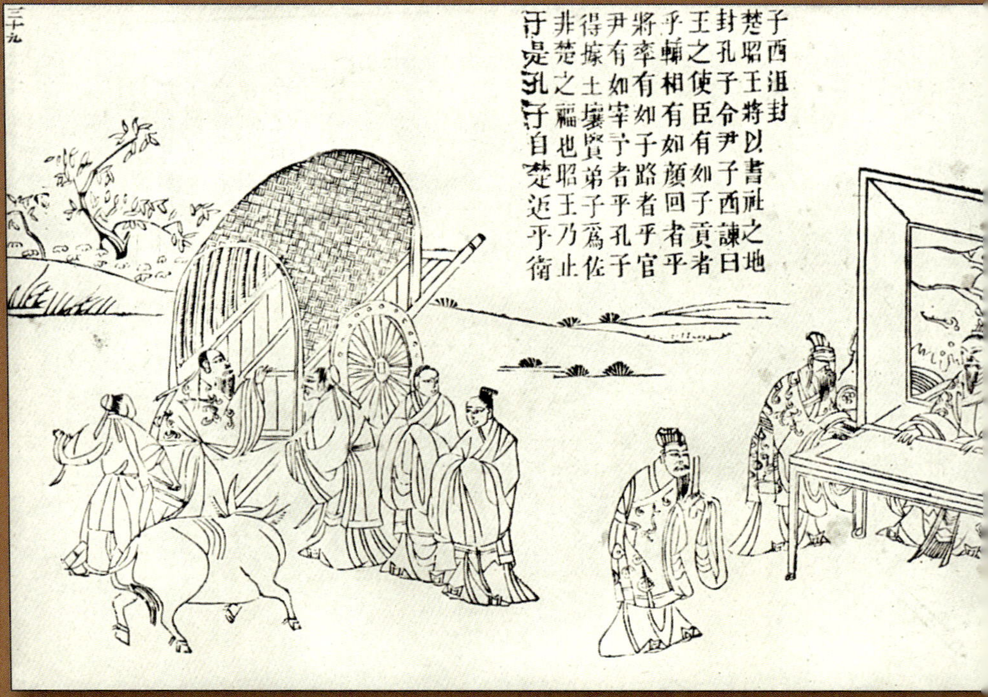

Confucius visits government rulers.

▼ Assassination attempt on Confucius

Beware of Your Enemies

On one trip, enemies tried to **assassinate** (uh-SAS-suhn-ate) Confucius. From then on, Confucius wore disguises (duh-SKIZE-uhz) while traveling.

Civil Service Exams

Based on some of Confucius's ideas, people take civil service exams today. They no longer pass government jobs from one family to the next. These exams test what people know about the government to find the best workers.

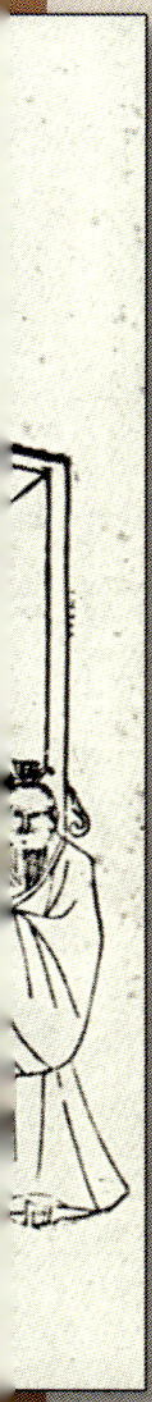

A civil service exam is given in China. ▶

Calling It Like It Is

Confucius traveled for more than 13 years. In that time he saw cruel **tyrants** (TIE-ruhntz) call themselves noble princes. **Assassins** (uh-SAS-suhnz) and thieves claimed to be good government workers.

Confucius believed in calling things by their right names. He called this honest language. In other words, Confucius believed in always being truthful. He told his followers, "If a ruler wants to be called a prince, then he must act like a prince." He said that one cannot rely on his noble birth. Rather, he should rely on his character.

Confucius said that a person should strive to love his neighbor. He wanted people to show respect to one another. To be a success, one had to live in harmony with others. This sounds similar to the Golden Rule.

◀ This image shows what homes looked like in ancient China.

The Golden Rule

"Treat others as you want to be treated." This is the Golden Rule. It was also taught by Jesus 500 years after Confucius lived.

Confucius Says…

"An exemplary person should be slow to speak yet quick to act." This is just one of Confucius's many ideas.

▲ Confucius tries to convince others to use honest language.

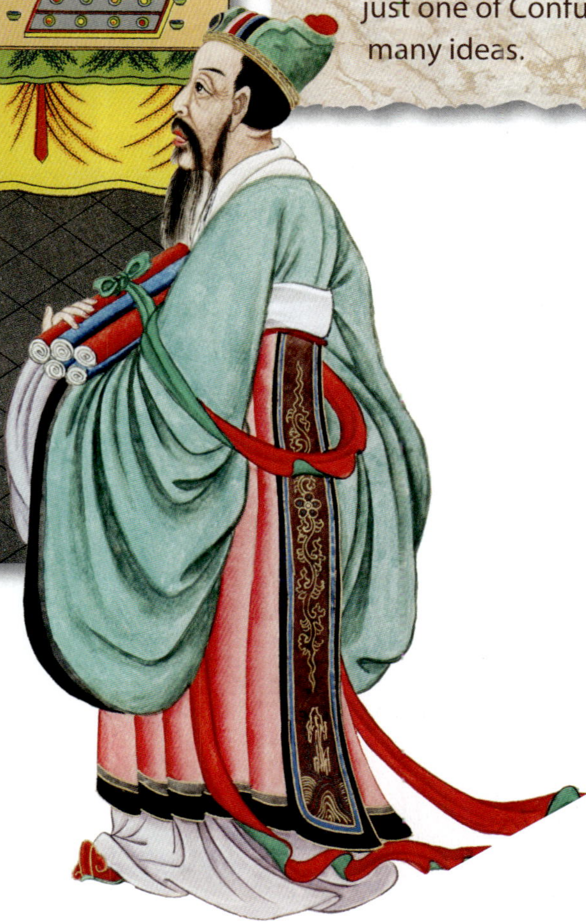

Dying a Failure?

After 13 long years, Confucius went back to Lu. He knew his dream of changing China was over. He never had the chance to work in a job of power like he hoped. Just a few years later, he died believing he was a failure.

His followers scattered all over China. They spread his teachings to all the people they met. This cost some of them their lives. The rulers in China were still not happy with the ideas Confucius had spread.

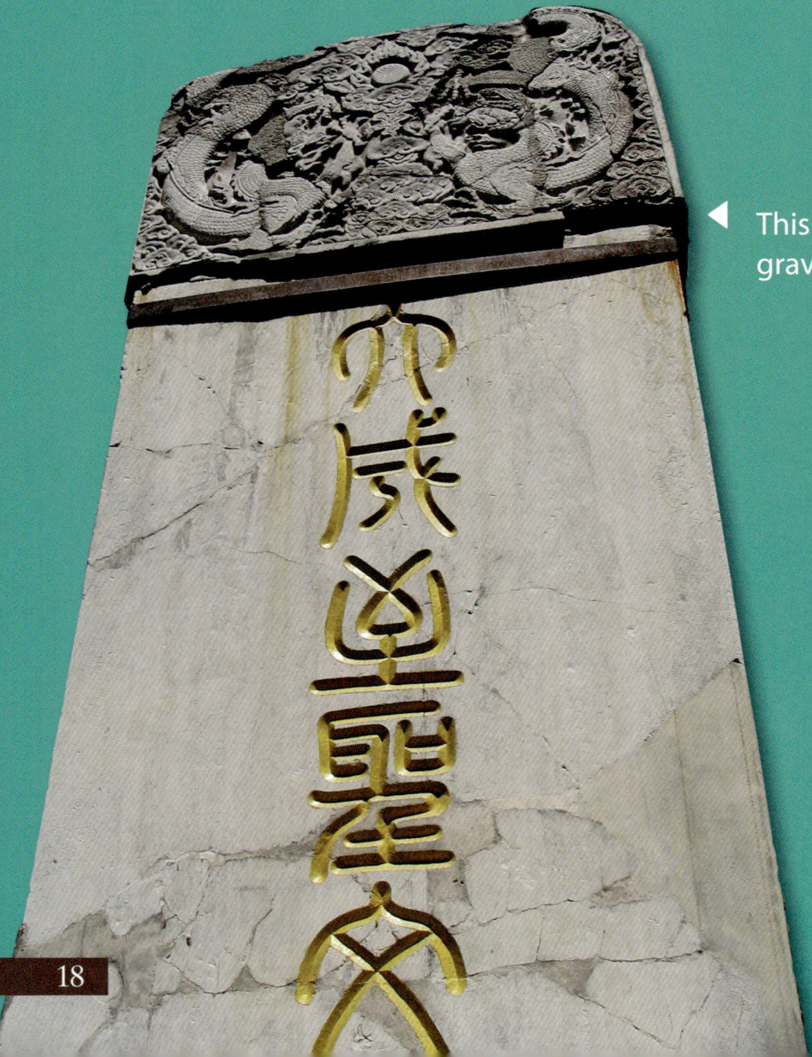

This is Confucius's grave marker.

Confucian temple today

Many think of Confucianism (kuhn-FYOO-shuh-nih-zuhm) as a religion. After all, temples have even been built in honor of Confucius. But, religion was not something he talked about. He did not spend time discussing death and the afterlife. Instead, Confucius focused on how to live in this life and how to treat others.

Looking Back

Today, people say Confucius was the greatest thinker in Chinese history. Unknown to him, he changed China forever.

Talking, Not Writing

Confucius did not write down his ideas. Instead, he talked about them. His followers later wrote down some of his sayings, and that is why we know them today.

A Disciple Named Meng-tzu

▲ Meng-tzu

Confucius had many followers called **disciples** (dih-si-puhlz). A man named Meng-tzu (MUHNG-DZOO) was one of the most important ones. He is also known by the name of Mencius (MEN-chee-uhs). He lived 150 years after Confucius.

Meng-tzu not only believed Confucius's teachings, but he took it one step further.

Meng-tzu said that the common people were the most important people in a country. The rulers were the least important. He said, "If the people see that the ruler is a tyrant, they should do away with him!" This did not sit well with the rulers of his day.

By that time, a new dynasty had formed called the Qin (CHIN) dynasty. The first Qin emperor set out to find Confucius's followers and put them to death. He completely outlawed Confucius's teachings. Some followers managed to escape, and they hid in hills and caves.

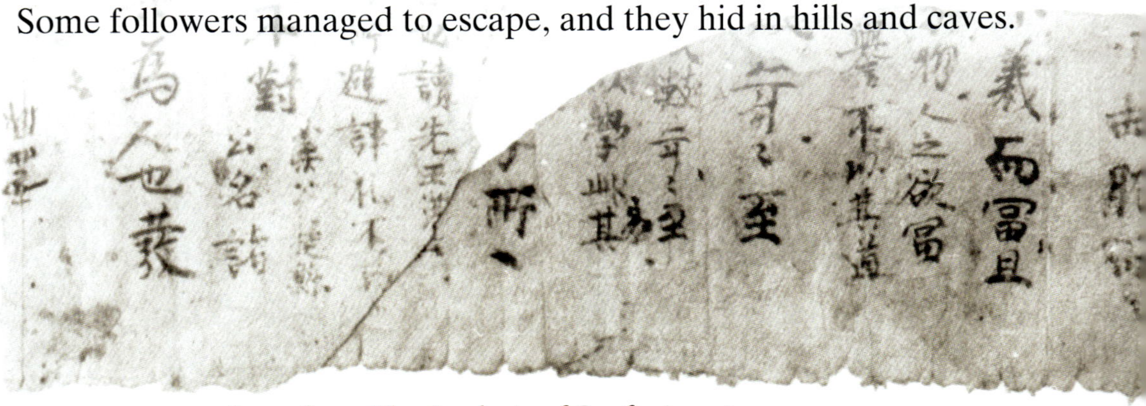

Page from *The Analects of Confucius* ▲

Qin Shi Huang
Qin Dynasty

A Book for Confucius

Meng-tzu helped collect and write down Confucius's ideas. He put them into a book called *The Analects of Confucius*. The word *analects* (AN-uh-lekts) means "sayings." You can still read that book today! A new version (VUHR-zhuhn) of the book is printed almost every year.

A Lot in a Little Time

The Qin dynasty ruled for only a short time, but they accomplished a lot. They built the Great Wall of China. They even created a writing system for all to follow.

Other Philosophies

Confucius was not the only person who had new ideas back then. Life in China was hard. Some thinkers believed that peace was more important than war. There were two other very popular philosophies: Taoism (DAU-izuhm) and Legalism (LEE-guhl-izuhm).

Taoism

A philosopher named Laozi (LAUD-zuh) founded Taoism. Confucianism taught a social way. But Taoism taught about a personal way. Laozi wrote *The Book of the Way and Power* also known as *The Way*. He wrote it for rulers, but many people used it as a guide for how to live.

◀ Laozi followed by one of his disciples

This book is filled with interesting statements. These statements seem to **contradict** (kawn-truh-DIKT) themselves. Laozi believed that a person could be strong by being weak. He said strong leaders can lead by not leading.

Laozi wanted people to live simple lives. He thought that people should not try to control their destinies. Instead, people should learn to be flexible about what happens to them. He compared this idea to water. Water yields (YEELDZ) to its surroundings. In the same way, people should yield to nature and to what happens to them.

Different from Confucianism

Taoism was different from Confucianism. Confucianism teaches rules about society and other people. Taoism focuses on a person and his connection with nature.

Zen

Taoism is rarely practiced in China today. But, Taoism has influenced other philosophies like Zen in Japan.

▼ Japanese Zen garden

Other Philosophies

Legalism

One more philosophy that came about in China was Legalism. Many people thought this philosophy had extreme ideas. Legalism said that people are bad and selfish. The only way to have order is to enforce strict laws. These laws came from a ruler. This ruler disciplined anyone who broke the laws.

Confucius said that the government should serve the people. Legalism taught the reverse of this.

Legalism was handy for harsh rulers in the Qin (CHIN) dynasty. They adopted it as their set of beliefs. In 213 B.C. one of the most **infamous** (IN-fuh-muhs) acts in Chinese history took place. The Qin leaders burned

▼ Terra-cotta soldiers

Leaders of the Qin dynasty burning books

any book that did not agree with their belief system. When Confucian followers tried to save their books, the Qin put them to death.

Great Wall

Find Those Books!

The next ruling family was the Han (HAWN) dynasty. Confucian followers searched for any remaining books. Legends say they found *The Analects* hidden in the walls of the Kong family homes.

Qin Dynasty

The Qin dynasty left two important artifacts. The Great Wall was connected into one huge wall during this dynasty. It is more than 4,000 miles (6,000 km) long. Also, the Terra-cotta Army was built. The army was supposed to protect Emperor Qin Shi Huang (CHIN SHE HWANG) after his death. Both of these artifacts tell people today about ancient China.

Later Confucians Borrow Some Ideas

▲ This symbol represents the Yin and Yang.

After the downfall of the Qin, the Han dynasty took over. People started to wonder how the whole universe worked. Confucians borrowed from other ideas to make their ideas stronger. They wanted their beliefs to appeal to more people.

One school of thought was the Yin and Yang. The yin and the yang are opposites of each other. They stand for all the opposites in the universe. The yin means female, dark, and passive. The yang represents male, bright, and active. The yin and yang balance each other and bring harmony. All that happens in nature does so because of how the yin and yang interact.

A Worthy Teacher

"If you study the past and use it to understand the present, then you are worthy to be a teacher."

-Confucius-

The Five Elements was another idea Confucians used. It meant that the entire universe was made up of five things: wood, fire, earth, metal, and water. These elements must balance to have peace in nature.

A Perfect Pair

Confucians during the Han dynasty said that a successful society relied on two things. First the people had to live in harmony with others. Second, they had to live in harmony with nature. Using Yin and Yang and the Five Elements, they brought these ideas together.

Confucius Says…

"Virtuous people are never lonely. They always attract neighbors."

◀ The Five Elements intersect to keep nature balanced.

The Greatest Chinese Thinker

China would not be what it is today without Confucius's teachings. These teachings have changed some over the years, but the basic ideas still exist.

Confucius thought a moral and just society came from two things: education and hard work. He knew

▼ This man is a descendent of Confucius.

people were smart enough to think for themselves. They should be valued for what they could do for their society. He wanted people to use honest language. Confucius also believed that rulers should earn their titles. They should be virtuous people who share power.

Looking back, we can see that others have followed these ideas. They are even found in the Declaration of Independence. If Confucius were alive today, he would be amazed. He died thinking he had not changed China. In truth, Confucius's honest language changed the world.

The Declaration of Independence

Thomas Jefferson wrote these words at the beginning of the Declaration of Independence. Governments "are instituted among men, deriving their just powers from the consent of the governed whenever any form of government becomes destructive of these ends, it is the right of the people to alter or to abolish it, and to institute a new government." These ideas are very similar to Confucius's ideas.

Confucius changed China's history.

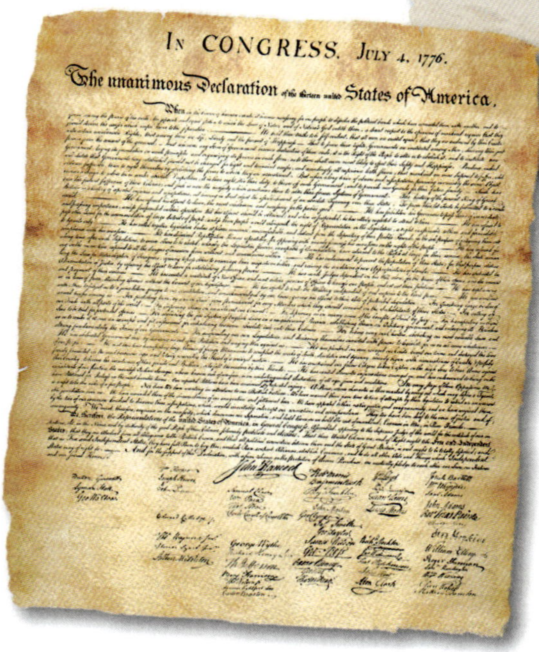

IN CONGRESS. JULY 4. 1776.

The unanimous Declaration of the thirteen united States of America,

Declaration of Independence

Glossary

ancestors—family members from long ago

assassinate—to murder someone important by a surprise attack

assassins—people who murder important people by surprise attack

chaos—confused; unpredictable

civil war—war between people living in the same country

contradict—to mean the exact opposite of

disciples—followers of a belief or cause

dynasties—family groups that maintain control of power for many generations

feudal—system in which peasants and farmers worked lands owned by noblemen

granary—a place where grain is stored

harmonious—to live in harmony or peace

infamous—scandalous, having a bad reputation for a deed

inherited—received from a former family member

morals—principals or rules that a person lives by

premier—the title given to the leader of China today

tyrants—a leader with absolute power

upheaval—to be chaotic and confused

virtue—goodness

Index

Image Credits

cover The Granger Collection, New York; p.1 The Granger Collection, New York; pp.4–5 China Photos/Getty Images; p.5 (top) Scott Rothstein/Shutterstock, Inc.; p.5 (bottom) Luisafer/Big Stock Photo; p.6 The Granger Collection, New York; pp.6–7 Tiberius Dinu/Shutterstock, Inc.; p.7 Mandel Ngan/AFP/Getty Images; p.8 Philip de Bay/Historical Picture Archive/Corbis; pp.8–9 Panorama Media (Beijing) Ltd./Alamy; p.9 Trout55/Shutterstock, Inc.; p.10 Burstein Collection/Corbis; p.11 (top) Bazuki Muhammad/Reuters/Corbis; p.11 (bottom) Kimberly Hall/Shutterstock, Inc.; p.12 Howard Sochurek/Time & Life Pictures/Getty Images; p.13 (top) Visual Arts Library (London)/Alamy; p.13 (bottom) Peter Turnley/Corbis; pp.14–15 The Print Collector/Alamy ; p.15 (left) Mary Evans Picture Library/Alamy ; p.15 (right) China Photos/Getty Images; p.16 Burstein Collection/Corbis; p.17 (left) Mary Evans Picture Library/Alamy ; p.17 (right) Archivo Iconografico, S.A./Corbis; p.18 Luisafer/Big Stock Photo; p.19 Tibor Bognar/Alamy; p.20 Luisafer/Big Stock Photo; pp.20–21 Bettmann/Corbis; p.21 The Granger Collection, New York; p.22 Chinese School/The Bridgeman Art Library/Getty Images; p.23 Allan Morrison/Shutterstock, Inc.; p.24 Rich Bartell/Shutterstock, Inc.; p.25 (top) Mary Evans Picture Library/Alamy ; p.25 (bottom) Wong Tsu Shi/Shutterstock, Inc.; p.26 Daniel Gilbey/Shutterstock, Inc.; p.27 (top) David Lee/Shutterstock, Inc.; p.27 (middle left) Rafa Fabrykiewicz/Shutterstock, Inc.; p.27 (middle right) Cre8tive Images/Shutterstock, Inc.; p.27 (bottom left) BelleMedia/Shutterstock, Inc.; p.27 (bottom right) Roman Milert/Shutterstock, Inc.; p.28 (left) Keren Su/Corbis; p.28 (right) Mary Evans Picture Library/Alamy; p.29 National Archives; back cover Yann Layma/Getty Images